MEMORY CHOSE
A WOMAN'S BODY

ANGELA M CARTER

Jeff,
Thanks so much
for your support. It
means more than
you'll ever
know. So glad
to know poets like
you

Angela

ISBN 978-1-936373-34-5

Published in the United States by Unbound Content, LLC, Englewood, NJ.
Cover art: © 2014 Brandy Somers Photography
Author photo: © 2014 Brandy Somers Photography
The poems in this collection are all original and previously unpublished with the exception of those listed in the credits page at the end of the volume.

MEMORY CHOSE A WOMAN
First edition 2014

To all the individuals that are and have been compasses and lighthouses throughout my life.

To my dear children, Eve and Nori: always see your worth and know that you were the creation of me.

To my husband, James: You are always home to me.

Table of Contents

Just Words

This story can't be smuggled away under a blanket.
It is a constant of mine,
debted ownership;
its meaning is clearer now than when it was first seen.
The seed deeper than my own physical being,
wilting into the stories that my children and foes will tell.
My words prove that there is no escape
from the many children of original memory—
where instinct echoes from a mother's bone to the growth,
into the legacy of many affected and ever-changed worlds.

On the Loose

Southern Virginia—where for years
I dragged my knees and feet upon her skin like a useless plow
ripping up the tides of thirsty dirt from the earth's store.
My skin shed scale by scale, peel for peel in the tired sun.
Those days whittled me into a ponytailed girl with a collection of sticks.
No. Barbie would not understand.

Wandering loose—
much like a stray unwanted runt;
repeated battles became permanent scars;
never did I win against myself.

The child I once was still resides in the forest
walking along the abandoned railroad tracks,
toting an empty case of a soul under her rough skin.
Her spirit furrowed and weary,
offering scaled lips that frame an uninhabited tongue.

Our children give her belief that she can drop her arms,
living through the hope in their trusting eyelids.
I try to lead her away, but she won't leave until I am able to answer:
why, why, why?
This is the one thing that I am still unable to do for either of us.

Splinter

I dream you back to take out a childhood splinter.
You say, "Look away if it hurts."
Your wrinkled hands pushing the thinnest needle into a cave the splinter built.
I adored the attention your fingers dedicated to mine,
and I prayed that you would find a trace of another thorn lodged under the
skin of my palm,
forever to be a puzzle you had to endeavor to solve.

I want to take back the moments of storm dorms crying at the presence
of a stranger,
when we lived for the rain to cool us and feed us all at once—
days when men were only husbands and fathers—
nights where a lover didn't rub the skin right off a woman's heart
during their morning escape—
mornings that I was not left alone to scrub my disappointment
off the wrinkled sheets.

If memory were to choose a body, it would be a woman's.
She would greet me in the cold hallway with a stuffed blanket.
Once I slept, she would sweep me into small piles of grainy pain
within the corners of the room
and place the most comfortable chair atop me as the liquor
bottles glisten in the windowsill.

I dream you back to take out a childhood splinter.
You say, "Look away if it hurts."
In some ways you breathed easier when I turned my teary eyes to the wall,
so that is what I'll forever do.

Country Life

That sort of life
ain't nothin' to sneeze at.
Each plant and crop
has a soul, and when lost, is mourned.
We smiled during reruns of the Porter Wagner show
as we shelled the beans with toughened fingertips.
Layers of skin peeled from the sun,
emotions only shown near a stiffened body—
my poetry imprisoned in boxes under beds;
dreams were for the greedy.

That sort of life
ain't nothin' to take on with a weak stomach.
Each memory lives longer than its human host,
ignored like a dog in an outside pen until after supper time.
Dinnertime, we said I love you with buttered everything;
the larger the meal, the more sorry we were—
we were always apologizing for something, it seemed.
The burnt car, a playground,
the trees, a jungle gym covered with thorn—
hangin' laundry outside in the dead of winter,
hugging a towel's body straight off the line like it was a newborn child.

That sort of living
ain't nothin' that can be understood by newcomers.
You must pass a kin folk's gravestone on the way to school,
and cry behind the trees on the way home,
return with purposely skinned knees to divert attention from the tears.
There are only the strong or lazy;
the sick, the weak, the different
are the highlights of the afternoon phone calls.
Years later my ears burn
reminding me of hanging tobacco on the farm,
throwing the tobacco worms in a bucket, with pity—
the 'bacca sticks splinter my hands, even in dreams,
and it is now the country life that I hide under my bed.

They Flee

I was made like this:
sensitive doll with scissors already keen on my hair,
a meaty doll with stolen underwear.
They sewed me up like this
and fixed me into much worse,
a toy asked to sit around its whole life,
too soon
to be without any worth.

I was made like this:
broken down for easy bites,
still legs that cannot take flight.
They broke me in like this
and asked that I stay
and I've sat here for years
waiting for your eyes to find me.

Over the Counter

I tore the label from the beer bottle
rested it underneath your buried nose
it waved without rhythm—
I believed each time the paper would remain still
and that your casket would need to be changed to reflect your limbs'
awkward outlines.

I became on my own
a $2-a-day child,
realizing, even then, your secrets cost more.
Cooked enough that I burned my identity from my thumbs
and didn't realize any value in the use of a washcloth—
they stay folded in the cupboard below the porn (that was used
by whom?) on the upper shelf.
My teeth bore 10 dark holes;
my future foretold many more.

There's a difference between being unwanted
and knowing you are unseen.
Passed along like the wobbling chair,
I, someone else's awkward seat forever,
I, my own unsteady posture.

On my birthday you begged that I return.
So I did and found a doll I wanted a year before
that I had since outgrown but pretended to need more than life itself.
You asked that I return to you to see
a new dance your limbs learned to recite on weekends only
and invited me wholeheartedly to stay Saturday and Sunday
if I still loved you.

I don't remember your eyes being open much.
I remember my feet being cold as I slept on a mattress
in the laundry room,
the washer always running but never having a matching pair of socks,
being 15 years old on a Saturday
so in debt with my past that I drank a bottle of cough syrup
as if it were a cure.

I dragged myself to the toilet,
shoved two fingers down my throat,
walked out of the bathroom, stumbling for a seat.
I waved a piece of paper under my nose to confirm life or death
and I couldn't definitively confirm one or the other.

I grew each day afterward, from child to bleeding woman,
washcloth to face, spine a little stronger,
wobbling seat of a chair to stronger legs of wisdom,
birthday girl to Santa Claus at Christmas.

Morning Glory

Gramma says I should not water the morning glories.
"As pretty as they are, they are a weed,
                    hungry and selfish;
they steal the sunlight from the beans."
"But you like roses," I say to her.
She does not respond.
I am told to pick the butter beans and snaps from the vines.
Moments of silence pass and I begin to wonder
if I, too, am a morning glory.

Telegrams

I delivered my mother's late-night letters
barefoot, across dewy grass and concrete
slugs and the fear of hissing snakes.

I was a proud postal worker,
Paul Revere's assistant,
a walking telegram of hope,
a sentence ending with a question mark.

I found her cursive fascinating,
the folded letters, ruled paper
decorated by a scorned woman's hand,
and I, the deliverer of choice.

She underlined what she would speak loudly.
The last letter that I opened stated:

DIVORCE

Just the Once?

Did it only happen once?
Show me how he did it.

And I showed you how he killed me
again
and again
I lifted my top and showed you
how the drying well began—
these droughts happen quickly
when the world ceases to turn.

I can tell you that I fade
when your lips are blue and split in two
and you sleep with my little secrets drowsy in your head
I know they knocked straight through
and looked at me through your pupils
and apologized for what they couldn't make your mouth say.

I can tell you that I showed you what he did
each day afterwards,
the teenage years of garage band sex
and the search party I never quit,
seeking love inside of "ribbed for her pleasure."

Did it only happen once?
Show me what happened.

And I showed you how I died the first time
how I looked up from that moment
and saw my skin as a dirty plain
that he, you, them, those, all could hurt me at least once;
but even then, I knew I only needed to die once.

Don't Play With Guns

I was handed a heavy handgun, at 9, maybe 10.
The handle, ivory and curved like a woman's hip
almost pretty to me
if a gun can be called that.
It weighted my arm enough that I could only point at my own toes.

He sat Indian style in the backyard and closed his eyes
liquor swirling in a clear glass beside one of his legs
and told me to aim and shoot as he pointed to his jaw.
Calmly, he told me how the gun takes charge of things,
and explained his plan, that this will be his end if I should choose.

I stood on the porch, confused and relieved all at once
that this man had given me a chance to rid my breast, my innocence, my family
of his gloom.
I remember knowing, by instinct, that if my finger presses, "this" would all end.
He waited for my thoughts and never moved and never pressured.
He only smiled.

Knowing nothing more than to set the gun on the concrete slowly,
my body heavier to the earth than the gun was to my hand,
I had chosen not to help all those that suffered
that my mama would still be black, blue, and broken,
and I would still have to wear sweaters to hide traces of my womanhood
in the summertime.

He opened his eyes,
walked up to the concrete steps,
picked up his ransom of a gun,
opened the back door,
and asked if I wanted a fried bologna sandwich.

My insides paralyzed
but my stomach heavy with fear
I nodded "yes," as I blamed myself. Because of my choice
I'd never eat anything fancier in life than that,
and I'd never be any more damaged if either of us were still alive.

Social Worker

She asked like it was nothing.
Trained well, she never directly asked the questions she needed
filled in on her paperwork
for her degree, for her own past wound.
Angela ... can I call you that?
    Nod. (I'm nobody)

Are you happy?
    Smile. (No)
Do you know who loves you?
    Nod. (No)
Has anyone ever hurt you?
    Shake head. (Yes)
I have things I'm scared of, do you?
    Spiders, I whisper. (Everything)
How is school?
    I get As. (The kids are mean to me)
You are a pretty girl. Do you think you're pretty?
    Nod. (Ugly)

Well, you seem to be a well-adjusted bright girl.
    Smile. (Did I pass for normal?)
      (She didn't say I was beautiful)
      (She will take me away)
      (She's leaving)
      (She's saying good-bye)
      (She's saying the court's requirement is satisfied)

(I bet she has an indoor dog. I bet she has photos on the wall. I bet she
can sleep easier with my answers.)

Real Kitchen Nightmares

Most fights occur in the kitchen,
where a few smiling faces are drawn by crayon
directly on the fridge and walls.
I've seen knives drawn for living flesh
and smelled more cigarettes
burning to their butts near the phone
than home-cooked meals.
Its closet is large enough for me to hide in
but not imaginary enough for me to disappear in.
When outside, I always look up at the kitchen window—
it is the pulse of the house,
with its own voice trembling,
always promising the next time I walk in
to be different.
But it always ends up with band-aids, stale bread,
and the smell of different types of smoke,
no longer a signal,
now the remnants of something completely destroyed.

The World Moved On

I knew much more than I should have as a child
and grew up more scared than any woman should be.
Each year rolls my easiness backwards.
There's too much I find buried
underneath the bones of my childhood.
The eyes of her remains never grew eager with death;
they are wide, open, and alert,
wiser than what has grown new of us.
The pupils have a painful stare,
impatient for a caretaker
to stare back at her as if she were whole.
She was a weed tossed in a southern sun-bathed bucket
that grew back quickly even through the plastic,
while on the other side, the world moved on.

Hunting Season

Grass-stained knees,
prickled fingers
bleeding from waking the sleeping thorn bush—
I meddled with the wonders
of the woods
where the beasts roamed
and the men showcased orange
flags of betrayal
along their mortal torsos.
The men are in a patient herd
while a deer looks up to the sound of
clicking branches below
a hunter's anxious foot.
I cry at the sight of its limp body
but smile as my father seeks my face
for a look of pride.

Remember to Throw Yourself Away

Saw my worth hit its own arms blue
like a red light flashing
that singes the skin
whether it glows or turns itself off.
I stored machine gun band-aids
that would be the bulls-eye for the next
canvas of pain.

Trash.
The room so small the mattress formed
a circle
and I slept in a cold "o,"
the closest thing I could find of you.
I gave up looking for warmth
and still settled for a walking corpse—
never seen a deadened heart walk so fast
from the loving in the living.

Graffitied barns
railroad tracks
bridges
that I made home for afternoons
more afraid of the turned eyes I knew
than the men that could turn my neck blue
and chase me all the way home laughing.

Trash.
The sour breath from never speaking
I could even feel the molecules in the air
choking me
bullying me
selecting me individually.

Who ever knew so many liked to kick trash around?
Never did I think that invisible me
would attract so many fingers and
unblinking eyes.
But I was trash
and I guess everyone wanted to remind me
that I must remember to throw myself away.

Hotel Song

Friday afternoon
we'd wait, noses to hot window pane
for the clicks and dust of your car
to disturb the driveway.
Hurry up before it overheats.
Hurry up because if I turn it off
I can't turn it back on.
Our weekend homes
had bibles in the drawer,
some I read, and many that I
used as an ashtray.
Sometimes we'd buy a pool for the night.
The blue water was our summer beach trip.
We'd dance underwater like we belonged,
like we were more alive when nearly drowning.
One night as I left the pool,
bathing suit still on,
a man offered me $250 to go back to his room.
I ran away like the hunted and screamed
all the way back to safety.
When I arrived back to the room it dawned on me that
it didn't matter how many monsters I ran from;
when I'm breathing I carry the scent of prey.

Womanhood

When it came
I thought I was the only one cursed with it;
rolled up washcloths, tissue, other pairs of underwear,
to soak up the signs of death.
Hid the evidence in the school bins that entire week
because I'd rather them see what
would be left of me in memory
than of what was leaving me.

Internal Compass in the Night

Tonight I have positioned myself at the lap of the world

I cannot release the stammer on my tongue
as bitterness churns in the pit of the fruit within me
that fell to soil so many sides of the moon ago. My

nomadic spirit argues with my security-seeking eyes
following sparrows of stars by thin strings. Galileo's

instruments, those mules; he could not see with or without them.
He envisioned the shape of moons before discovery.

O, how my instincts have stopped trusting; my pupils have stopped adjusting.
My bones recite a lock-kneed dance so reflexively. Each

night I look above to the tiny dots of compasses
and hear their hums above the buzzing and stings of the earth's tent.
They lead me back to the home that exists safely within the cage of my ribs.

What's the Matter?

The responsibilities that we are gifted are heavy.
Upon the moment our mother's pregnancy test is wetted
we are already whole, already a plus and a minus, a caressed cell
or a legless elephant
depending on whether she is resting in front of a fireplace
or warming her hands by fire under a bridge.
We are her incentive to be more
and why she can only be but so much.
Was I a reason?

It's such a responsibility
to have so much effect on things you cannot foresee—
emotions of others that we never fully feel
tears we see but never warm us—
I say to my children: "I wish you knew more about your roots
as your roots have grown taller than my own tree."

The responsibility that empathy can never surface like mountains
on our skin,
but our masks insinuate our emotions' end.
Has your heart reached its depth of understanding
enough for you to give away your next to last dollar?
Did your tears fall enough that I know you care?
Can a husband place a bet on human life
that he will forever be the roots and tree of me?

Even if we all never made it past the minus
on the pregnancy stick,
we are the reason for so many whys.
Am I a reason?

Angelina, Ballerina

My feet on top of your hunting shoes
dancing to Hank Williams Sr.
Around in a circle I twirled with you
in your bright orange vest and my
tomboy hair,
in that moment, long with perfect pin curls.
You looked down at my gleaming eyes
and knew there were some lights inside me
that were no longer.
You called me Angelina, Ballerina when you were playful,
you wanted my voice to remain innocent and small,
easy to trick out of those moments where you must sit
in surrendering silence.
It is comfortable silence that I sought in a husband,
needing a stubbled beard scratching my aging cheek.
I wanted you to use both eyes to see my lips pronounce:
*Daddy, you could not have protected me from those things
and I cannot protect you from who those things made me become.*

Fear of Weeds

Under where the concrete cracks
the depth of what has become dirt gasps for sun
and sprouts a weed.

Are we so sensitive and overly aware of loss
that we shy away from it,
so inspired by life that we do not taste the rain on our tongues
during a storm?
We do not create a new chapter in our own stories,
unable to see that with a step into the rain the weed we sprout
might bloom a morning glory.

Southern Drought

The children are always lost
but never said to be missing
as long as they return with clean hands
at the neighbor's barbecue
before the charcoal fully burns.
They are wild
like the summer azalea mornings
and oblivious like the gathering bee;
death does not linger here,
life does not explore further land.
The children thrive in a way
only the wind of a southern drought
can understand.

Days Like That

I overheard a townsperson say that they found a body
floating in the lake.
The shooter, her unlawful Mr,
had christened a gun that had decorated the house
like a thinning Christmas tree stuffed in a box
in the summertime corner.

The man she gave herself to that day
was beside her, I was told,
floating face down,
retrieved like thin tree limbs before time could turn them cold.

I saw them both a week before,
we ate hamburgers,
and sat comforted by the sound of frying grease.
I remember a sweet man and a raspy woman
whose hand held both a cigarette and a beer.

I have heard him called a killer,
I have heard her called a runaround,
and I have heard the devil lives in all of us.
He found his way to them both that day.

The devil waits patiently for days like that.

White Picket Fences

Unmysterious, symmetrical
a newly built fence
surrounding land like a wedding dress
keeping its family pure in its bond to the home—away from venturing;
shielding strangers from the pitch of the midnight screams.
Bouquets of envy planted along the walkway
as if to say,
this is the perfection that you should expect in our home.

"Beware," the girl says to me as I walk by,
"We have a dawg."
I step back, not because of fear,
but because these types of homes do not have welcome mats
placed outside the fence,
but instead the mat can only be seen by those invisible enough
to be invited to the front door.
Visibly broken people are not welcome.

Moths

Many things I'm sure I don't recall,
second by second;
however,
some are so well defined and jagged they spear through my feet
and create a kaleidoscope in front of my eyelids
that never shakes or makes that
satisfying clicking noise as it's being turned.

I remember Halloween.
You returned from rehab
me with a Pound Puppy mask,
making a dog's whimpering noise,
wanting you to see me play the part well
and partly wanting you to hear how it feels when butterflies realize
they were seen no more than as moths
            a nuisance even in an unused attic space.
The whimpering began as a dog and became much more human
as the night went on.

I would smile and pull the mask down afterwards
the muscles on my face rested to slumber after a long while
of no response from your own.
I forfeited at the starting line of a promised new beginning.

I remember the phone call weeks later,
expected by my ears, unprepared by my blood,
your arm broken,
ribs cracked,
your scalp without its hair.
And I, in tears,
of sympathy and jealousy
that your pain had a name, a color, a face
and you chose not to see the face of my culprit until
he beat you black and blue.

When the Water Goes Cold

The bathroom reminds me of
        head lice
        pink calamine lotion on skin
        and the disgust of nakedness.
My body, in a bath.
Sitting in a small amount of lukewarm water
not knowing how to clean away the grit atop my skin.

The window open just enough
that our dog barks as it reacts to the captivity of the chain's length.
I dared not rush outside and calm him each time, knowing
that he will be more sad if I show him, temporarily, what lies beyond
a shelter, food, and water.
Eventually he stopped whimpering and learned to stop searching
for more grass
just as I did.

And if I'd had a car
if I'd had freedom to share,
he and I would have both found our grass
because no one understood me more than he did.
I believe he barked not just because he saw further flight—
he did so because he knew I, his best friend, could not.

Bows & Blades

There's something about shoes that make a home;
yours went missing far before you ran away
and mine were made over and over with laces
knotted and tied with force over the door
nowhere to pull the ends.
I grew with arms waving to you from behind
the bowed prison,
and you added more bows for the outside world to see.
I would jump up on the counter over the sink
and play with the faucet while I looked for you to arrive
over the yonder, even feet away looked so green
your car parked only for small moments;
smile and I knew you would stay longer,
cry and you would have toes curled facing the nearest door.
When was it that the bows became knots,
the knots could not be found
but with age my mouth grew a sharp blade
that only seemed to shelter me and never affect another?

Where Were You?

I bet they can't remember that same moment.
I would have done anything to have been there
instead of behind the doors I leaned against,
to have uncovered my mouth
when strangers asked what was the matter.
Do they appreciate the beauty
of resting in their sleep,
swimming in mundane memory,
the feeling of a summer's peach on their lips,
saltwater shriveling their toes?
I would have done anything
to have stared up at their light-polluted skies
and painted dreams on a blank canvas,
to step backward and steal
their forgotten time
if it would erase what I recollect of mine.

Periwinkle

Pink tongue peeking out between your pressed lips in concentration
as we sat on your bedroom floor:
me, the awkward girl with bucked teeth and frizzy hair,
you always said I was pretty,
even when my first crush told me I was not.

Even at your funeral
no one could speak of you without the corners of their mouths turning upward,
pews of loved ones wishing for your return.
I sat toward the back
remembering your face as the last I saw of you,
staring at your matured smile printed along paper,
face of a woman with the smile of an innocent child.

While we were coloring
you pulled one crayon out of the box and said,
"I like this one. Periwinkle. Not blue, not gray, sort of in between, but prettier."

In my adulthood, you still live.
You helped mold me.
What I have passed on to my children is partly you.
In your voice I tell them that they are beautiful.

Even now, as I sit on a bicycle
it brings me back to a place I was with you riding over
cracked sidewalks, passing failed crops, swimming in the murky pond,
quarters clinking and clanking in our pockets
so that we could share a candy bar.

I like to think of myself as the color periwinkle,
not blue, not gray, sort of in between, but prettier,
sought by your eyes, even when others would have passed me for red.

Quiet

She is too quiet, they used to say,
her breath sour from lack of opening the mouth.
not even her tongue ventured to the chapped upper lip.

Stepping onto the school bus,
book bag strap broken,
she walks to an empty seat,
ties a knot to join the useless frayed fabrics

unaware
that a boy is betting on her not to speak.
He moves into the seat next to her.
While the others watch in anticipation,
his hands, uninvited, grope where they shouldn't.

Her silent tears,
red face,
shamed by those who watch but do not help.
We are going to tell, they say.
The girl, called to the school office,
speaks.
She is told it was a misunderstanding.

She returns to the world and the eyes
hands over chest,
whispers clouding her ears,
to hear one particular comment:
It wouldn't have happened if she wasn't so quiet.

That she.
That her.
That unfortunate I.

The Broach

My last snakeskin was left at the boarding gate of a plane
and what was left underneath would do.
The world,
scary, torn, unmet even when some of it was unseen
to an ant that never strayed from its reliable, unsavory food.

Some I met along my travels said they've never seen one wear pain
like it was a shiny thing,
like it was a broach with no face, pinned atop my coat,
and that I welcome the old backstabbing friend with a forgiving grin,
"God must've turned his head one moment
and the wicked pulled your hand."

And my response:
If that is true,
God must wake to my face and even dream of me
in his slight waves of slumber,
he must've named my feet after the lighthouse near the shore.
There is no pain where there is not something virtuous to work toward.

I Suppose

I suppose I wore a little thing of a dress many times that summer,
my long, disproportioned legs making the hem fall too short.
In fairness, when I was asked what I did to deserve the attention,
no words built upon my tongue to amount to any reason.
Guilty, I was,
my echo of memory still remains a slur.

I suppose I laughed too heavily, snorts and all,
spit fell under my bottom lip as I did.
I thought I should love even if hesitant
because you sat up straight only when he came around.
Your lips became feminine and loose and would make it closer to
my forehead;
they never fully landed.

The acting,
the bruises,
the "she" taken from the inside, the "it" of me
never pained me as much as the silence that followed.
It is my skin that I have shed
but my mind that has grown layers of nonflowering seeds that
even I can't seem to profit from.

I suppose because I was old before I was young
I've silently given men permission to take my skin as their hide.
The beat of worry and damaged goods easily detected
in advance
to their plan of breaking me apart anyway.
Validation, to the hunter, I breathe.

What began as a back rub one afternoon
became the front rub,
became drilled holes in the walls for easy view,
became doors that would not lock,
became cars that could not be driven,
became me yelling out loud in pastures of no scenery,
became me being pulled into the backseat of a school bus
and shushed

when I told the principal and the teacher about the boy,
became me losing my tongue,
playing dead
until there was nowhere to play anymore.

I suppose I did long to be wanted,
liked it when anyone ran their nails softly over my scalp and ear,
relished the way some listened to me.
But don't we all when we know of nothing
that could happen beyond?

Scars Return on New Skin

Fighting myself
talking over my own voice
racing my own pulse
this is the first I've seen
the mousy brown-haired girl
with the gapped front teeth
that THE MAN paved over
with his hands,
picking her prematurely from dry soil
only moments before the rain could have come.

Melancholy worn like a derby hat throughout her adulthood,
comfortable underneath, but displaying a raveled bow,
hospital socks underneath newly polished shoes,
bristled legs with scarred knees
from where she shaved, at 9, in a waterless bathtub.

She does not hesitate in showing her wrists,
they as original as a new mirror picked up by the blind.
It's her voice that's been censored,
removed,
handled without care,
stolen,
needed,
forgotten,
and now deemed good
because it ceased to exist.

Woman at the Auction House

"I ain't givin' nothin' away, darlin'," she said as she pressed her
stub of red lipstick to her lips. She turned her head to the side,
her shoulders still straight. "Don't look at me so sad, cause ain't
nothin' easy 'bout me, shugga. My skin may be sold, but this here
the real 'pensive stuff ain't got no dolla signs on it."

I did not believe her at the time, her eyes looked easily swayed.

Every time the door opened we could hear the auction men, their
voices boxing to be heard over one another's in that land of musk
and lust for things that may or may not work where we weren't
allowed, no child no woman nobody no corner warmer. I never
had hope that I would grow a voice enough to enter those doors.
Or any others. Even then I knew that although our purposes were
different, our jobs were to wait for others to want us.

"Some men can't stop hunting, even afta they own the fur an'
antlers. Darlin', you'll know it one day. And ya might be standin'
somewhere like this tellin' some little girl the same thing and she
givin' you that same look you givin' me. You'll see. These corners
can give a woman less bruises and more luv than that out there
can. A ledge, winda, bed, drivin' a car, and on the floor—
we've all got our corners shugga. Even you."

Justifying

Ever so loud your tongue waved,
loose and uncaring
toward the throat of my being
and what I once loved about myself
escaped from its cage of certainty.

I don't have say in some parts of myself—
the cells of personality placed wildly by condition
in uniquely patterned boxes
with wire attached to my ring finger,
holding my life ransom since my youth.

Segregated from my own instinct
before introduction of nurture,
I show muscle in my eyes
but my heart weeps and loudly cries;
worth was never stuffed behind my seams.

If you had ever been me,
if you had innocence stolen before it could be worn in
you'd understand fear of any dark road or room
any unlit area in life leaves me suffocating.

There is a siren with every man,
every dream,
every assumption that one makes,
every silent eye.
It tears at my fancy threading all the way to the bending bones.

Soldier

It has been a while since I have seen my fist,
seen my body in soldier's stance:
I'm blank-faced and toes curled
over a repeatedly cleaned toilet,
my body turned into an opus of pain.

My two warrior fingers surrendered
to my tongue and she, the tongue,
demanded they follow her to the back of the throat.

She whispered that my soul has sunk to the bottom of our sea
and that I need to search day and night to find it,
the more I give the more I will understand.

I release my soul, in pieces.
Day by day it suffers the abusive warmth of swallows
and I know it is full and grown once again
and what I have retrieved will return momentarily.

Like a seashell in a violent sea
she whispers in my ear: "You can never get rid of me."
Pleasing the throat, the road to all that is physically me,
I pull to the leaves, never to grip enough to retrieve the roots.

Is what we have survived all we are?

I am a lamb
with wool singed by
the devil's bully.
I have won the battles
but exit without tough skin.

Cute meat
windowsill scenery,
how prissy I am while I fall onto my ribs to find milk,
panicked because the world is nearly a dry well
as I search for worth to add to it.

Desert bones, unidentified footprints,
no one searches for a lamb when they see the mother content—
they accept easily
a starving lamb's belly full in the last tug of breath.

To Forgive but Not Forget

Somewhere the steps stopped producing
and my legs stopped uprooting
and I realized now my number would never be called. Never.
And even f it were, where is there to go that offers any soil, sky,
or bite enough for my angered teeth?

I want to be the sweeper, the mother, the one with bruised hands
because pain has brought me the purity of a daughter's stare
and the fruit of a nurtured weed.
Winding roads, my only perch in life's nest,
a nest built from cigarette butts and shreds of an off-brand cereal box.

Even with the rotten fist of a man on my breast as a child
I still sing to my beloved and uncover my skin to him.
Even with a maze of disappointments
I want for no other dwelling
Than the journey that has led to this intended home.

Gut Instinct

There ain't no money to be made in poetry
or sanity to find among the words.
Strap your soul
to ink-filled fingers
and let them
tidy the gut of your pulse.

That is priceless and costly, all at the same time.

Two Beasts

I keep warm from burning memories,
from feeding my new fires with
mountain peaks of stacked vodka labels,
canoes created from rolled cigarette skins,
bibles that housed condom bookmarks.
Over the top of them are now
shiny poetry book sleeves,
labels from $30 lipstick tubes,
newfound innocence,
betting slips where I bet for myself to win.

There's an ultimate need in us all
to ride the bull in youth, but walk away without him,
think of him as a thrill ride we left when we ran out of quarters.
I rode him out of my own war, and, because he was all I knew,
I set him free inside to crash about within my
library of thoughts and memories;
he's just as unhappy as I am.

I cannot set him free—
where would he go? Who would we have?
People don't carry quarters anymore,
they carry shiny debit cards.
People don't carry hearts on their sleeves,
they hide weapons under them.
We cannot continue to grow anew
when a sad beast, mad for wings,
can never be as free as she dreamed,
and the bull never tires of seeking redness.

Red, found in every corner, every uneasy laugh,
every bout of sadness, every flashback,
every day.
He seeks what I endeavor to hide
and I run from him never knowing if all
he is searching for is the same as me:
more than winning, more than destroying, wanting to live—
simply facing life is all we both might need.

Little Black Bird

Somewhere a bird hates her own beak,
despises her own color,
obsesses over it,
seeks reflections in windows and
side car mirrors.
She cannot fly from her own voice box,
so she punishes herself.

No worms.
No chirping.
Too many worms.
More worms.
She must get rid of the worms.
No chirping.

Somewhere I am a bird.
Not far.
Very close.
Right here.
On this page.
Fighting to accept my own chirp.

To Be Taken With Food, Water, and a Smile

Pretty pills, you have your leash
pulling me into grace, dragging me, emotion-first, into safety.
Pink and white, oval and round, should be elementary.
But reality is arduous when realizing
that only without myself
can all damage be superseded inside.
Remind myself to breathe when it is time to gulp you.
Let you take away my word's unique dances
my tears and mouth waterless—the seesaw of salt and sugar.
The choice of freedoms: concocting speech, narrowing the
hallway of fear,
wetting the crumbs I've dropped along the way.
I chose daily to swallow a creation that extinguishes
the very fever that has always represented me.
Silence is perceived as a type of contentment
so I dare not speak
about how I lost myself months ago
on a Monday morning—
93 days, 186 gulps ago.
I premeditated a kidnapping
but no one is searching.
They like this new smiling face much more.

What We Really Hide in Paper Bags

Gain and loss happen
side by side they race
like blood in a vein,
a simple unbreakable machine that
a pregnant woman welcomes while painting walls blue
and the mother of a sick child shuns
by closing every door behind her,
but one day she is too late. Too late.

Death, a bully that won't pick his next prey,
he lingers with enough time for everyone.
He can be found by the smell
in the waiting rooms, the bedrooms with bedpans
and he waits at the back of the lunch line, just when you
thought your last quarter was safe. It was not.

Happiness is folded inside a handkerchief in security's pocket,
found in the glance a child donates,
the arm a dad places on his daughter's shoulder,
the wag of a dog's tail,
the ring that slides on a finger longing for warmth.
It is now cold.

We rest our hearts in paper bags
but tear tiny holes in it,
just enough to show everyone that is is not a weed.
It is contrary,
that it beats, is, in fact, true,
even if we don't believe it ourselves.

Claws

I ran to a new land
caught red-faced and black-handed
out of organic breath, strapped down, by choice, on a plane.
Breathing the remnants of the devil's laugh,
caught by a thread of life
only seconds before being stolen back by America.

America gnawed at my ankles
a hungry floor
she pained for the bone above the shoe
until she reached the hinge of knee,
ventured upward
and even the heart was not enough of a treat.

Sanity, a washing machine run during a child's nap,
mine ran at midnight,
dirtying the already canopied eyes and deafness.
The land did not mourn the loss of me
or notice the clawed fingerprints I left on the plane window
as the English sky engulfed me whole.

It's only when I became no one
that I was able to become someone.
I withdrew, a woman,
and returned to America as a wide-eyed child.

Migration

If the soul would always know when to migrate—
if it were like our hand's sensitivity to burn and chill—
life would be simpler and skillful.
The timer is always broken
for us to retrace our steps
and paint over the red of pain and white of boredom,
creating a lifetime of masterpieces of memories, wants, and regrets.
We are all in constant search and migration for our callings to be heard,
travel, never cheap or without risk.
But we are annual flowers, pretty for the short while
that we fill another's eye
only to wilt with time whether or not our purpose is achieved.
Our wants slightly step, stumble, graze knees and learn to walk, then run,
then pace ourselves.
We have earned the stability of knowledge.
The bell is always calling for another chore to be completed,
another sidewalk to be swept,
so that our journeys may be easier, lead us to new adventures
until our loved ones read "Here lies … ."
We never truly lie down in life or death;
once we are found by others we are still in search of ourselves.

Songbird

I slept,
released from the daily stages
my spirit running freely across
the stitches and untethered seams of the earth.

My feet tore at the ground
bordered heaven's gate
and awoke to the sullen world
of desire, superficial hunger and greed.

One day in July
a voice awakened me and sealed my eyes momentarily.
Up until that time the caged bird ran
in circles scratching to be free.

Peculiar nature of survival,
it, neither he nor she, is an exotic beast
that has moistened its tongue of freedom,
that was once dried in my depths.

The quench of thirst that bird was born with
has been filled three times over
and will sing until its earned death.

The Second Floor

The second floor is for those of us still salvageable,
the youth in madness' lifespan, bipolar, unilateral depression,
throwing up our Snickers bars after group therapy.
We speak of the third floor as if it is unattainable,
but the staff look at us as if we are only one step down
from the ledge,
like they could just throw a bone and we'd follow.
We, the Breakfast Club of the damned, socially pathetic, the denied,
damaged and drowned from the neck up,
still hope for the beating thorn below.
Crazy. Loony. I've only been me, how do I know if I am?
What is normal?

Overly medicated until I see thieves that aren't there
while I soak in a bubble bath filled with the warmth of fear.
Let's try the blue one, gray one, white one, now the pink.
Put the notebook down, dear girl, misery should not be allowed any ink.
We may leave at the end of the day,
no permission required to pass the exit door.
We can bathe our babies,
we can sleep without others at fear.
I would bet we all lay there, every item on the checklist checked
except for ridding our minds of the need for constant survival,
thoughts that battle every waking moment,
an insurance claim,
barely making it,
scrounging for pennies of happiness that end up down drains
and mostly counterfeit.

Regretfully Mine

The past's path
still exists through this time
reminding me of journeys lived and passed.
Along the bristled bushes rests warm sand,
tangible but settled into its final rest.
Memories stir its dust and wake regret.
When the buzzards swarm,
I know it was right to carry on.
I drag my flesh into the night forgetting this past day.

Thanks for Not Understanding

If it ever happens to you
(which I hope it does not)
you will look at me differently.
You'll swallow your own salty tears out of a foggy glass,
the mirror will reflect two eyes, prematurely dead.
At night the sheets will feel too close,
so intimate that you will believe the fabric is trying to choke you.
You'll call me, recognizing my reflection in your own.
You'll ask
how'd I handle the pitiful stares
from even the neighborhood dog.
If it ever happens to you
(which I pray it never does)
you will need patience that even religion cannot give.
You will need to remember to groom your nails
and brush your teeth twice a day in case you decide to smile.
Each day will be a year, dragging you behind the miles
of each minute uncaring and deaf to your pain's moans,
you giving blank stares at your own injured body.
But these things you may never understand
(and I hope that is always the case).
I used to want someone to understand me
(and now I only wish that no one ever does).

Everyone Looks Calm While Sleeping

A disorder, he called it.
The doctor gave it skin and premature front teeth,
slapped it on the back with precise force,
and watched it nap with a sly smile
in front of the neighbor's peek-hole in the door,
lured it back home with a pink pill when it ran away.
Swallow the pills at breakfast, lunch, and bedtime
it must be attached like a Siamese memory—neither I
nor the pills have purpose with the other.
Warm mouth or dry capsule,
it no longer needs to scratch away at the crumbs in the alley later at night,
it weeps loudly for all to hear at the kitchen table
or when a visitor opens the cabinet to find a glass for water.
In a replica red-light window, I twirl with dejected eyes,
known as the one that used to be wild-eyed, unpredictable,
the one that dangled my legs from the side of the bridge
free of the cost of life
and made you forget your own memories and hiding places.
Now that reasons are known
everything expected, accounted for, in the right queue.

This Is Why Heaven and Hell Exist

We would have stolen anyway
but blame it on the barrel of the gun pointing at us.
Knowing it was loaded
what others think suffices.
Hope, it screams,
like a barrel resting on the temple of our being,
comforted by it warming to our skin.
We never reach our depths if we dare not fall to our knees,
and even a fully loaded consequence does not make us plead.

Tattoo

My first tattoo, at 18,
was a rebellion, meaning that I wanted to remember rebellion.
My second was a confirmation of my voice.
The third was an expression that I will forever be free
while realizing freedom is not always an offered choice.

It is those things that even ink can't show,
lines that would sway like a crazy hand if I described it.
So now I have learned that it is those things I tried to prove
through my skin, seeping into my own bones,
even the lost memories of aging can't misplace its effect or make it move.

Thanks to Wine

I fell asleep on the carpet and let
grains of short braided cloth make homes within the ridges of my face. I
lay mentally deformed and careless, staring at an old
photograph of myself on the wall.

Walking Photographs

Bare-bodied we all are, weaknesses glistening like sweat in the moonlight,
we, standing, squatting to an inch of a mile
abusing air, but never appreciating it.
Surviving off of framed moments,
only hunting the pose of the turned-up mouths
before lipstick and ties are removed.
I wish to forgive myself and embrace
a life unstill, that moves feverishly day and night.
Wrecked into truth, I would simply be garnished with refined gloom
transparent symmetry of underappraised worth
that I accept can never be fully tuned.

Final Abandonment

The past's path
still exists through this time
reminding me of journeys lived and passed.

Along the bristled bushes rests warm sand
tangible but settled into its final rest.
Memories stir its dust and wake regret.

When the buzzards swarm
I know it was right to carry on.
I ignore my past skin, which has aged more than what is new.

Sometimes There Is No Choice

Simplistic design
of the soulful mind:
it digs and tortures
every vessel that has comfort.
Threads of trust stretched thin,
into its own tidal rhythms,
the ocean's hands sweep
all that is foreign away from its skin.
In boats of hope
we dine on the angry sea
until it wakes us in nightmare,
taking us underwater with its last forceful tone.

Why don't you write about something happy?

I leave the happy for my mouth
for the teeth to show their shape;
for my legs to seek the playground of earth
for my chin to not want to rest on my palm.

I leave satisfaction for the laughs
for empathy
for the dreams that others have
that I dare not want my expressions to ever spoil;
for the need of us to trust our guts while our feet cannot touch the ground.

I drop desperation to the floor,
and let it bounce back on the paper
so there are no subcultures in my spoken words
no sharpened glass left from the mirrors I have broken that will hurt you
due to me seeing my double chin.

I create a dialect of comfort
so your mind does not have to dissect what your eyes show it;
sadness is the part I want engraved when this other of me is not left
to make you happy,
to make you care.

I, Misery's Company

I was attracted to the misery in you,
you were familiar.
Our hearts blended in melancholy,
rooting into one another,
into the same rotten soil.

No blooms, only roots that conjured weeds,
making miles of bleak mundane scenery—
gray paradises.
Each and every day we were afraid
that if sadness left there would be nothing more
than the silences we couldn't fill with happiness,
and the misery that needed company once more.

Renovation From a Dresser's Point of View

Have I crossed myself
even walked through my old self
the naive nomad
now a refined gravel road dweller
no ending in sight
and our rearview mirrors the same,
turned up a little too high for our eyes to reach.
The echo of my feet on this uncarpeted floor
scares my old self
into the dresser
left alone in the center of the room
with its arms crossed
one over another
wanting the girl out
and for me to place my new clothes in it.

The bed is now able to rest.
In the shed it sleeps,
relieved and aged,
never wanting to be set up again
even in the best of worlds.
It prays itself to the floor
where it hopes to live forever.

The bricks still intact
but the wood behind it thin,
replaceable.
The shingles' corners escaped and hammered over
time and time again.
The house, it lives much like a nanny to those it housed.

*They have grown up, my babies. They have grown up to be different
than I would have wanted, but the silence of renovation sure is
sweeter to the ear than the sound of their fury.*

Some Things Never Change

The skin below my eyes weeps to my bone
begging for it to be carried 'round a little more.
In the corners of my days, I stood,
sadness' fingers intertwined around the
ten babies of my two hands
and loneliness never seemed so strong
or the grip of failure lasted so long.
There is no pill to swallow
that will shush all the hollow
and so I write it out in blues of all shades:
almost plum, almost a gray, periwinkle.
They melt like crayons.
The colors overlap and, although once unique,
begin to cry out as if they were all once the same.

Butterfly in Reverse

I had wings.
Once.
They seemed no different
than human hands
until plucked.
Reluctantly.

Along the mantelpiece,
beside a twenty-dollar bill,
the world, smut-stained,
neither touchable
neither of them mine.
Gone.

Butterfly in reverse,
ill pupa,
inch worm,
at half an inch.
Until I forgave.
Wings aren't required to fly.

Against the Current

Two weeks before, I visited you.
I remember the ammonia smell,
knowing it covered more than it
ever prevented.

You offered me hard candy,
everything you had near your hospital bed.
I'm proud of you, darlin', hug, hug, hug,
and I left thinking your body was bluffing again.

Two weeks later you were hanging on,
but your body had left long ago,
your breath still paddling against the current,
and your face had lost all of your spirit.

Near midnight, I called the nurse,
asked if she would place the phone at your ear.
I could hear your last labor in breath,
you never were a woman to rest when tired.

I told you I was sorry and grateful,
that I knew you were too,
it was OK to say good-bye
because we'd talk more another day.

The following day, 11 am phone call,
I was in the bath, as many tears as water.
You were gone.
Resting.

Why are we surprised by death?
He does not lurk, he smiles brightly.
We convince ourselves that there was no pain—
when it is ours alone—now, it is only me that is alone.

Breathe

The simple cures are deadly—
nothing quick is quick.
If we bleed out, we die,
if we empty our stored tears all at once
an unfulfillable drought would exist inside.
Nothing is free. It's attached to threads of insecurities
weighed down by sad balloons that are greeted
by grit floor. No, it costs to want and need.
It costs just to be
and I'm out of the correct change,
out of water to fill up my own dead sea.
But sometimes I close my eyes and can be
as dark as I dream,
exist as a half, happily,
no one able to understand my language
of indecision.
I envision my tired soul
dancing as it one day leaves, singing:
It costs to want and need,
it repays once we are set free;
her heart did all the work,
and fought to stay clean,
but was never given rights to eternally breathe.

Poetry Saved My Life

In times that I am able to be
I call and write
to something higher than I.
I must be who I am for a reason
I was stitched
into these imperfect squares for a reason,
and my visionary mind built to
conceive these words
I now write.

Poetry, you beautiful, intense creature:
You saved my life.

Grunge Days

We talk backwards
about how "us youngins" escaped
the devil's teeth one million times,
how one time we outran
death on the railroad tracks
and left drugs in the 90s.
We were lost together
sharing a mile-high abandoned nest.
As adults, we manifest our former selves,
how daring we were,
how the things we once did could have ruined our lives.
Now we know there's a whole world
wanting to feel touched by something
and we still aren't open to being reached
by anything but doubt.

To Heathrow or Bust

You might as well be dead to me. Gone.
What more is out there than what is here?
Didn't it all follow you through the air,
and travel the ocean's floor—
wait at the terminal, smirking proudly,
wet and dripping,
with a sign in hand:
WELCOME HOME!!

Does it still hate me when you are a world away?
Or has its pulse weakened by the miles?
Does it breathe vengeance more steadily?
Or did it die since you weren't around to mother it?
I demand you come home.
I returned home years later,
to "home," a lost land.

Forgiveness or bust.

Positively Negative Pregnancy Test

To me, you were real:
curly brown hair and cliff-hanger eyes.
I know that look you'd give me
straight out of the womb.
I knew you were in there,
a new planet forming
in a desolate universe.
I could feel the craftiness
of skin being formed.

But I just found you you will
never be born.
You never were.
Planet Pluto, now just a moon.

At Christmas there would have been
an extra stocking to hang,
laundry day, more socks to sort.
There is no you,
or as much of me as I thought.
No feet.
No toes.
No face.
No fingerprints.
I'm burying you before you were,
but can't justify a stone.
Your name would have been Noah
or June,
I liked Ezra for a day—
I thought of so many names
that all could be you.

But I just found out you
never were;
you are not.
Like Planet Pluto, you became just a moon.
Good-bye my sweet, dead June.

Hope

Finally the glass has no streaks.
The sun can peek in
and needle its rays through any imperfections in my eyes,
touch the cold meat that still pulses behind its skin.
Why does it still move when no one can see?

The day still carries on
when my mind stops on one thought
and I re-run your streak of gray hair through it like a cleaning
cloth
that never takes the dust away.
Even in a dream do you also have me within you?

The bed never seems still.
It carries me along my entire day
and back through pastures of choice,
only to negotiate them all into my self-believed worth:
whatever someone is willing to give me.

Marriage

Can't you just see the child in me standing,
open heart to the air,
swirling the hem of an old t-shirt around my finger,
waiting in the woods for you to show me what home means.
Please brand me permanently with care,
though I realize the good may sting a little.
Why wouldn't it when I have become numb to the bad?
I'm covered with marks I cannot remove,
cannot cover with color,
cannot magically wish away in fairy tale books
because I have only allowed myself to process
the pages of conflict.
Give me a story,
a castle,
a prince,
singing wildlife,
a glued-on slipper,
read me the first page to the very last.

Symphony of Index Fingers

Only one man has cradled all I am,
all the others untuned me
chipped away at my ivory keys.
Clever how they pulled every working
uncanny hair of extra breath from my lungs
so they could get closer to the true sound of discomfort.
Each time the sound grew more precise
the pulls would no longer be lazy
and would tug at things the naked heart could never fully see.
And so the ear adapts
and requests more.
I pulled myself into hiding behind my pupils,
away from any fruit I grew and nurtured within,
unconscious of how foul, rotten my garden became
in any sunlight that lingered.
Happiness placed a trigger alongside my forehead.
And the gun smoked far before any choices were offered.

I. Am. Strong. Now.

Muscle is shown in my eyes

and squints when I see a red cloth in the corner of my sight.
Throughout the years I've reglued and chiseled my perceptions,
always finding that I've dug a hole in advance to bury my own self.
I needed no enemy—I never let myself grow taller than any other.
I was always horizontal, feeding on the dry dirt.

But behold the miracle of water: I allowed the rain to fall through the
cracks feeding persistent weeds. Cue the blooming morning glory.

Muscle is shown in my eyes.

The Meaning of Life Is to Create Life
(to Eve and Nori)

My labor, its fruit
the flowering seeds of a limp weed.
You can't ever take away
any scar of mine,
but instead, cover it completely with the trust you have in my arms
as I hold you.

Your open fists of ten swimming men
that paddle and float slightly to reach me,
that walk your legs learned on their own
unstable and fidgety
now steady and planned,
these things mesmerize me.

Unpainted heart, I want to cover you in eggshell white,
discard any future black and gray,
mold the faltered world surrounding us as if it is papier mache.
I see the girl inside me
peeking out the corners of your eyes,
that child waving, playing, fulfilled through your own skin.

You mesmerize her.
You mesmerize us.
My life,
eggshell white.
You were my first breath,
my first answered cry for the milk of life.

Taillights

When I thought it was done
it returned,
laid across my bed
leaving me without ample sleep.
The tragedies of experience form
the uneven legs of the bed
and tip me closer to the world
before I am ever rested.
I'm handed delicate objects
into my shaky hands
and I should feel lucky,
but I was built to be scared.
I am pointing taillights forward
and there's not enough light to see by,
only a warning sign I point to:
Caution: Please don't hurt me.

Sweetly

As I breathed the cool side of the pillow over my face,
I wondered what color my children's eyes would be.
I dreamed of hand-written letters from a secret admirer,
conjured a man with black hair and safe eyes.
I reminded myself how every experience would be a poem at least.

Dusting

Emotion should not be treated like a stomach.
It does not growl or heave when it needs.
Instead, it folds into new shapes, stops digesting on cue,
emerges into new accents, loses its tongue.
It can live on nothing at all—
what was never given cannot be craved.

Do not try to lead one that was never led.
We find our way, content without the eyes of nurture.
We create our walkway by chiseling the rock with our nails
and scraping the fingerprints off our own fingers.
It is through instinct that we become.

Experience makes us individual.
Each moment has its place on the shelf.
Each upcoming moment will rely on whether you choose
to dust these moments
or simply hide them in a locked box
for another to discover in your path someday.

Protector

They look forward to
birthday hats and candles.
Twice a year
I watch as
my girls' eyes widen
only an inch away from
each naked flame.
Somewhere distant
I wait and squint
for their wrong steps
into the world's
painted dungeons
and the princesses' graying hair.
I may be able to save them
if I could only stop weighing
them down with my own fear.

Memory Chose a Woman's Body

You and I have grieved more than any death;
the deathbed swallowed by the floorboards.

We have saddled more soldiers than wars have needed;
let's return them home to rest.

The years have rewound to my first years more than the film will allow;
the picture unusually sharp for its age.

The years have been hell-bent on recollecting certain terrible days;
we could create some good ones, still.

Our memories live in their own universe;
and this one has sometimes failed because of it.

Memory chose a woman's body;
she's tired and wishes to go softly in her sleep.

Memory requires blood too hot to live so wholly;
and forgiveness has shaded my entirety into lukewarm acceptance.

She needs our regret in order to live;
and I require our growth to exist without her.

Nothing Will Ever Be New Again

I choose my soul blind
and use old drapes of memories to mask the colors I elect not to see.
The girl I was taped my inhibitions on the outside panes
of my bedroom window
and every once in a while my nails scrape a fine tune
across the glass to try and reach them.
But that naive tadpole, once inside, knew little of the raw meat
that hangs from a woman's ceiling
and drips on her white cotton sheets as she rests for the new day.

All the choices I made with greatest intentions
mean I can never be new;
the hands I choose to hold walking into a dark room,
the selectiveness we encourage when remembering
and telling why we returned when we wanted nothing
more than to run away.

There is a realization that all this must seem quite sad,
but I relish the crevasses that dine on my skin,
and the nine months of belly that is from overeating trust
folds inside a body that houses aged senses.

No, we cannot ever be unseasoned.
It was only when I tossed my life like a rock
that I stopped chipping myself repeatedly like a delicate figurine.
Nothing can ever be restored to its nativity, but it may renew.

Forgiveness

If you do love me,
I need you to accept these words as if they were the note left on my deathbed,
that every punctuation is a bleeding wound
with an outdated tourniquet that causes harm.

Please accept that my mouth will not be closed even in bereavement,
that I can no longer be sensitive to the lowering of brows.

Pretend that in my last breath you would take your finger
and instead of shushing my lips you would search for my tongue.
You would pound me back to a beating heart,
beg me to speak until there is no breath left in my stomach,
not even enough to whistle through the imperfect gaps of my teeth.

Pretend that this moment exists now.
Say to me that you did the best you knew how and it fell short of being
enough, that there is no longer a law in your eyes that upholds silence.

I forgive
you the years spent breaking each individual finger of your own demon's hand
not realizing his other hand was strongest and pulling me away.

I forgive
you for watching my body, close enough,
not knowing my soul had been missing for years.

I forgive myself
for not loving myself enough to not accept merely breathing as living.

And it is here, this moment I need in this poem,
that I close my eyes and my lips part to your ear.

I will find the blanket that we covered the past with
and move it to new ground.

Your arm will stretch around my shoulders to soothe my opposite ear,
my ear, as small as it was years ago,
can accept the intentions of your aged hand as being fully reborn.

Mama

The permission I waited for,
the confirmation that
I am more than skin, teeth, and nail—
it arrived.
There is a heaven encased in our future
and the hell of the past fades slowly,
its deep violet smoothes into soft gradients of purple
now all delivered as a small girl
after many deaths.
Even the skin of this new body has heartbeats
and changes our own primary tunes.
I ran through Virginia corn fields
and London streets
calling your name
with a drunken mind
fiery legs,
exhausted voice.
And years later,
you call for your missing baby;
I crawl home.
I arrived home, a woman you didn't recognize,
but accepted and anticipated
like a baby weeks before its eyes meet yours.
And this makes all of what I have lived
worthwhile.

Woman Child

I was the waiter.
I waited for the built-up noise of my one-millionth silence
to be acknowledged.

I was a creator.
I fulfilled their need of risen cheeks
before they could gnaw on the woman child within.

I was the secret-keeper.
Opposite ear permanently closed,
one eye winked its warnings to passers-by.

I was the cleaner.
I rocked heavy, limp bodies.
I hid their liquor bottles before they awakened to my cries.

I was the trusted.
Slammed my self-worth on their sorrys.
Keep this secret, they said.

I was the woman child.
The heart, tissue paper thin,
with cement and chains, to protect the skin.

I was the runner.
Born from the fastest beast of life.
I ran before I could crawl.

I am the survivor.
I am the dreamcatcher.
I am anything I choose to be now.

ANGELA M CARTER has been a writer since the age of eight. What began as an escape from the events of her childhood became a way of life. Angela writes about subjects many people are uncomfortable

talking about. Each of her poems is its own story, yet they all carry the same message: silence is not golden.

Born and raised in a Virginia farming town with a population of fewer than 280 souls, Angela moved to England for several years only to find her memories followed her. She returned to Virginia with new-found confidence and a voice. She has been speaking with that voice ever since.

Angela is a wife and mother and she believes that had it not been for poetry she would not be either of those things. She believes that poetry saved her life.

Publication Credits

Special acknowledgment is made to the following publications in which some of these poems first appeared, sometimes in different forms:

Our Stories Untold: It's Never Too Late: Butterfly in Reverse
The Phoenix (Eastern Mennonite University, 2011): Internal Compass in the Night
Premiere Generation Ink: Silence
The Word Ocean: Hunting Season, Southern Drought
Worst Week Ever: Internal Compass in the Night, Rubbish, Thanks for Not Understanding, To Heathrow or Bust

Selected Titles Published by Unbound Content

A Bank Robber's Bad Luck With His Ex-Girlfriend
By KJ Hannah Greenberg

All That Remains
By Brian Fanelli

At Age Twenty
By Maxwell Baumbach

Assumption
Earthmover
By Jim Davis

Before the Great Troubling
Our Locust Years
By Corey Mesler

In New Jersey
By Julie Ellinger Hunt

Just Married
By Stan Galloway

Painting Czeslawa Kwoka: Honoring Children of the Holocaust
By Theresa Senato Edwards and Lori Schreiner

Riceland
By CL Bledsoe

Saltian
By Alice Shapiro

The Pomegranate Papers
This is how honey runs
Wednesday
By Cassie Premo Steele

31774735R00059

Made in the USA
Charleston, SC
28 July 2014